DO MATH WITH SPORTS STATS!

BASKETBALL

Stats, Facts, and Figures

BY KATE MIKOLEY

Gareth Stevens PUBLISHING

Please visit our website, www.garethstevens.com. For a free color catalog of all our high-quality books, call toll free 1-800-542-2595 or fax 1-877-542-2596.

Cataloging-in-Publication Data
Names: Mikoley, Kate.
Title: Basketball: stats, facts, and figures / Kate Mikoley.
Description: New York : Gareth Stevens Publishing, 2018. | Series: Do math with sports stats! | Includes index.
Identifiers: ISBN 9781538211298 (pbk.) | ISBN 9781538211311 (library bound) | ISBN 9781538211304 (6 pack)
Subjects: LCSH: Basketball–Juvenile literature. | Basketball–Statistics–Juvenile literature.
Classification: LCC GV885.1 M55 2018 | DDC 796.323–dc23

First Edition

Published in 2018 by
Gareth Stevens Publishing
111 East 14th Street, Suite 349
New York, NY 10003

Designer: Samantha DeMartin
Editor: Kate Mikoley

Photo credits: pp. 4–29 (paperclips) AVS-Images/Shutterstock.com; covers, pp. 1–29 (pencil) irin-k/Shutterstock.com; pp. 4–29 (post-its) Pixel Embargo/Shutterstock.com; pp. 4–29 (tape) Flas100/Shutterstock.com; pp. 3–32 (graph paper) BLACKDAY/Shutterstock.com; covers, pp. 1–32 (bleacher texture) Al Sermeno Photography/Shutterstock.com; covers, pp. 1–29 (clipboard) Mega Pixel/Shutterstock.com; covers, pp. 1–29 (formula overlay) lolya1988/Shutterstock.com; covers, pp. 1–29 (index card) photastic/Shutterstock.com; cover, p. 1 (women) Vico Collective/Alin Dragulin/Getty Images; cover, p. 1 (arena) EFKS/Shutterstock.com; p. 5 Icon Sports Wire/Icon Sportswire/Getty Images; pp. 6, 7 Bettmann/Bettmann/Getty Images; p. 8 Past Pix/SSPL/Getty Images; p. 9 (WNBA today) Icon Sportswire/Icon Sportswire/Getty Images; p. 9 (first WNBA game) Todd Warshaw/Getty Images Sport/Getty Images; p. 9 (background) seksan wangkeeree/Shutterstock.com; p. 10 Es sarawuth/Shutterstock.com; pp. 11, 18 Aspen Photo/Shutterstock.com; p. 13 Orlando Sentinel/Tribune News Service/Getty Images; p. 15 Harry How/Getty Images Sport/Getty Images; p. 15 (background) leungchopan/Shutterstock.com; p. 16 Mike Ehrmann/Getty Images Sport/Getty Images; p. 17 Ronald Martinez/Getty Images Sport/Getty Images; p. 19 Paul Natkin/Archive Photos/Getty Images; p. 19 (background) reShoot 69/Shutterstock.com; p. 20 Rob Carr/Getty Images Sport/Getty Images; p. 21 Lisa Blumenfeld/Getty Images Sport/Getty Images; p. 22 Pool/Getty Images Sport/Getty Images; p. 23 Steve Dykes/Getty Images Sport/Getty Images; p. 24 Al Bello/Getty Images Sport/Getty Images; p. 25 Tim Clayton - Corbis/Corbis Sport/Getty Images; p. 27 Elsa/Getty Images Sport/Getty Images; p. 29 Sergey Novikov/Shutterstock.com.

Printed in the United States of America

CPSIA compliance information: Batch #CW18GS: For further information contact Gareth Stevens, New York, New York at 1-800-542-2595.

CONTENTS

Words in the glossary appear in **bold** type the first time they are used in the text.

TIPPING OFF

Two opposing players stand at center court, waiting for the game to begin. Eight other players, four from each team, surround them. An official throws the ball into the air, and the two players jump for it. This is called the tip-off or jump ball. The first player to hit the ball tries to tip it to their teammates. If they're successful, their team has gained **possession** of the ball.

KNOW YOUR STATS

Statistics, or stats as they're often called, are an important part of basketball. Stats show how well a player or team is doing. Some of these numbers are simple to keep track of. Others require some math to figure out.

Every basketball game begins this same way. But what happens next changes from game to game. The goal is to score as many points as possible, but the numbers on the scoreboard aren't the only ones that matter.

THE AREA WHERE THE TIP-OFF HAPPENS IS CALLED THE CENTER CIRCLE. JUMP BALLS CAN HAPPEN THROUGHOUT THE GAME FOR OTHER REASONS, TOO.

THE BEGINNING OF BASKETBALL

James Naismith invented basketball in 1891. The sport got its name because Naismith used two peach baskets as goals. Originally, the baskets were not open on the bottom, so a ladder had to be used to get the ball out after every basket was made!

Naismith's game quickly became popular across the United States. Over the years since it was invented, some parts of the game have stayed the same, but many things have changed. Point values changed, and official rules were put in place about the size of the court and the lines on the court.

NAISMITH WAS A GYM TEACHER. HE CAME UP WITH BASKETBALL WHEN HIS BOSS ASKED HIM TO CREATE A FUN INDOOR GAME THAT COULD BE PLAYED DURING THE WINTER.

THE NUMBERS GAME

IN MOST **PROFESSIONAL** AND COLLEGE BASKETBALL GAMES, THE COURT IS A RECTANGLE 50 FEET WIDE BY 94 FEET LONG. CAN YOU FIGURE OUT THE AREA OF A BASKETBALL COURT THIS SIZE? REMEMBER, THE AREA OF A RECTANGLE IS **CALCULATED** BY MULTIPLYING THE LENGTH BY THE WIDTH.

ANSWER ON PAGE 29.

By 1936, basketball had become so popular around the world that it was included in the Olympics. In 1946, two groups joined together to form the National Basketball **Association** (NBA). This quickly became the major men's professional basketball league in North America.

AN OLYMPIC EVENT

Basketball was played in the 1904 Olympics, but it wasn't a medal event and was only considered a **demonstration**. The 1936 Olympic basketball event was held outside on a sand court. It rained during the final game. The United States beat Canada 19-8.

In 1976, women's basketball was included in the Olympics. In wasn't until 1996, however, that a group of officials from the NBA decided to create an American league for women. On June 21, 1997, the New York Liberty and Los Angeles Sparks played the first Women's National Basketball Association (WNBA) game.

first WNBA game

the WNBA today

KEEPING SCORE

In Naismith's game, the team with the most baskets at the end of the game won. Today, baskets can be worth different amounts of points depending on where the ball is being thrown from and why the ball is being thrown.

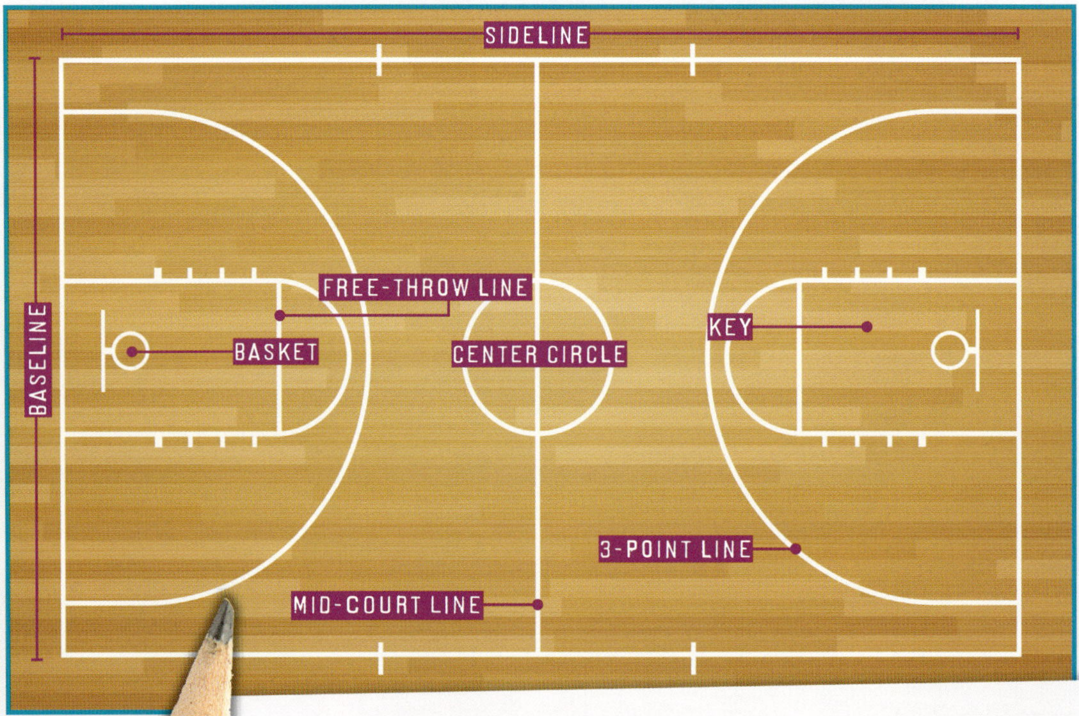

THE NUMBERS GAME

TODAY, BASKETBALL COURTS ARE SYMMETRICAL, MEANING THAT EACH HALF OF THE COURT HAS THE SAME LINES AND IS THE SAME SIZE AND SHAPE. WHAT LINE SHOWN ON THE DIAGRAM ABOVE REPRESENTS THE BASKETBALL COURT'S LINE OF SYMMETRY? ANSWER ON PAGE 29.

The big arc in front of each basket is called the 3-point line. As the name suggests, any shot made from behind that line is worth 3 points. Any shot made during regular play from inside that line is worth 2 points. If the opposing team commits a foul on you while you're shooting, you get to shoot from the free-throw line. Free throws are worth 1 point.

BASKETBALL COURTS DIFFER IN SIZE DEPENDING ON WHO'S PLAYING. PROFESSIONAL AND COLLEGE COURTS ARE USUALLY BIGGER THAN HIGH SCHOOL COURTS.

WATCH THE CLOCK!

Basketball games can be shorter or longer depending on whether it's a high school, college, or professional game. Games can also be longer if they're tied and go into overtime. College games are usually broken up into halves. High school, NBA, and WNBA games are broken up into quarters.

In the WNBA, quarters are 10 minutes each, so full games are 40 minutes. In the NBA, quarters are 12 minutes each. A standard NBA game is 48 minutes. This is the amount of time on the clock, but with time-outs and other breaks, games last much longer than this!

THE NUMBERS GAME

IN PROFESSIONAL AND COLLEGE BASKETBALL, EACH OVERTIME PERIOD LASTS 5 MINUTES. IF THE GAME IS STILL TIED AFTER THE 5 MINUTES, ANOTHER PERIOD IS PLAYED UNTIL THERE'S A WINNER. AT THE END OF 3 OVERTIME PERIODS IN AN NBA GAME, HOW MANY TOTAL MINUTES OF PLAY HAVE THERE BEEN? ANSWER ON PAGE 29.

$48 + (3 \times 5)$

THE SHOT CLOCK LIMITS HOW LONG THE OFFENSIVE TEAM HAS POSSESSION OF THE BALL BEFORE THEY NEED TO TAKE A SHOT. THE NBA AND WNBA BOTH USE A 24-SECOND SHOT CLOCK.

FIELD GOALS

In basketball, a field goal is a basket scored on any shot other than a free throw. These can be worth either 2 or 3 points. Field-goal stats are important because they show how well players and teams do at the most important part of basketball—scoring points!

Field goals play a part in lots of stats in basketball. Field goals attempted show the number of times a player or team has tried to score. For this stat, it doesn't matter whether the ball went in the basket or not.

GIVE IT A SHOT

Even though they don't always score points, attempted field goals are still important. The more often you try to make a shot, the more shots you are likely to actually make. The other team may be better at shooting, but if you make more attempts, you might be able to beat them!

Chris Paul takes a shot!

FIELD GOAL STATS DON'T USUALLY TAKE INTO ACCOUNT HOW MANY POINTS EACH BASKET IS WORTH. THAT'S WHY POINTS ARE AN IMPORTANT STAT, TOO.

Field goal stats get a little more complicated when it comes to figuring out percentages. A player's field goal percentage is the percent of attempted shots they've made. To calculate this stat, you divide the number of field goals made by the number of field goals attempted. This stat can be shown using the actual percent, or it can be shown in decimal form, usually showing three decimal places.

There is also a stat called effective field goal percentage that takes into account how many of the field goals were worth 2 points or 3 points.

Kawhi Leonard attempts a field goal.

IN THE 2016–2017 SEASON, DEANDRE JORDAN PLAYED 81 GAMES WITH THE LOS ANGELES CLIPPERS. HE FINISHED THE SEASON WITH A FIELD GOAL PERCENTAGE OF .714, OR 71.4%, ONE OF THE HIGHEST SINGLE SEASON FIELD GOAL PERCENTAGES IN NBA HISTORY.

THE NUMBERS GAME

IN DECIMAL FORM, A PERFECT FIELD GOAL PERCENTAGE IS 1.000. THIS IS INCREDIBLY RARE FOR ANYONE WHO'S PLAYED MORE THAN A FEW GAMES. IF A PLAYER'S ATTEMPTED 100 SHOTS AND MADE 48 OF THOSE, WHAT DECIMAL WOULD REPRESENT THEIR FIELD GOAL PERCENTAGE? ANSWER ON PAGE 29.

$$\frac{48}{100}$$

GET SOME POINTS!

Compared to other sports, basketball is usually considered a high-scoring sport. Some games can end with teams racking up more than 100 points each! Occasionally, an individual player even scores 100 points in a game. In 2012, a college basketball player from Grinnell College scored 138 points in a single game!

WHILE STILL RARE, AN INDIVIDUAL PLAYER SCORING MORE THAN 100 POINTS IN A GAME IS ACTUALLY MORE COMMON IN HIGH SCHOOL BASKETBALL THAN IT IS IN THE NBA!

In 1962, while playing for the Philadelphia Warriors, Wilt Chamberlain set the NBA record for most points scored by one player in a single game. Chamberlain scored exactly 100 points and helped the Warriors beat the New York Knicks with a score of 169-147!

THE NUMBERS GAME

BECAUSE SOME SHOTS ARE WORTH MORE POINTS THAN OTHERS, A PLAYER CAN MAKE MORE SHOTS THAN ANOTHER PLAYER AND STILL HAVE FEWER POINTS.

IF A PLAYER MADE 8 THREE-POINT SHOTS, 4 TWO-POINT SHOTS AND 2 FREE THROWS, HOW MANY POINTS DID THEY SCORE? REMEMBER, FREE THROWS ARE WORTH 1 POINT. ANSWER ON PAGE 29.

$(8 \times 3) + (4 \times 2) + (2 \times 1)$

HELP YOUR TEAM OUT

Basketball is a team sport, so not all stats are about being the one to make a shot. Multiple players help make shots happen. Assists show passes that directly lead to a shot being made. The official in charge of keeping score decides if the pass counts as an assist, so there's some judgment—and sometimes some **debate**—that goes into it.

Like most stats, assists are kept track of per game, per season, and for a player's entire career. Players can rack up thousands of assists throughout their careers.

John Wall makes a pass.

JOHN STOCKTON HOLDS THE NBA RECORD FOR MOST CAREER ASSISTS. IN HIS 19 SEASONS WITH THE UTAH JAZZ HE HAD 15,806 ASSISTS!

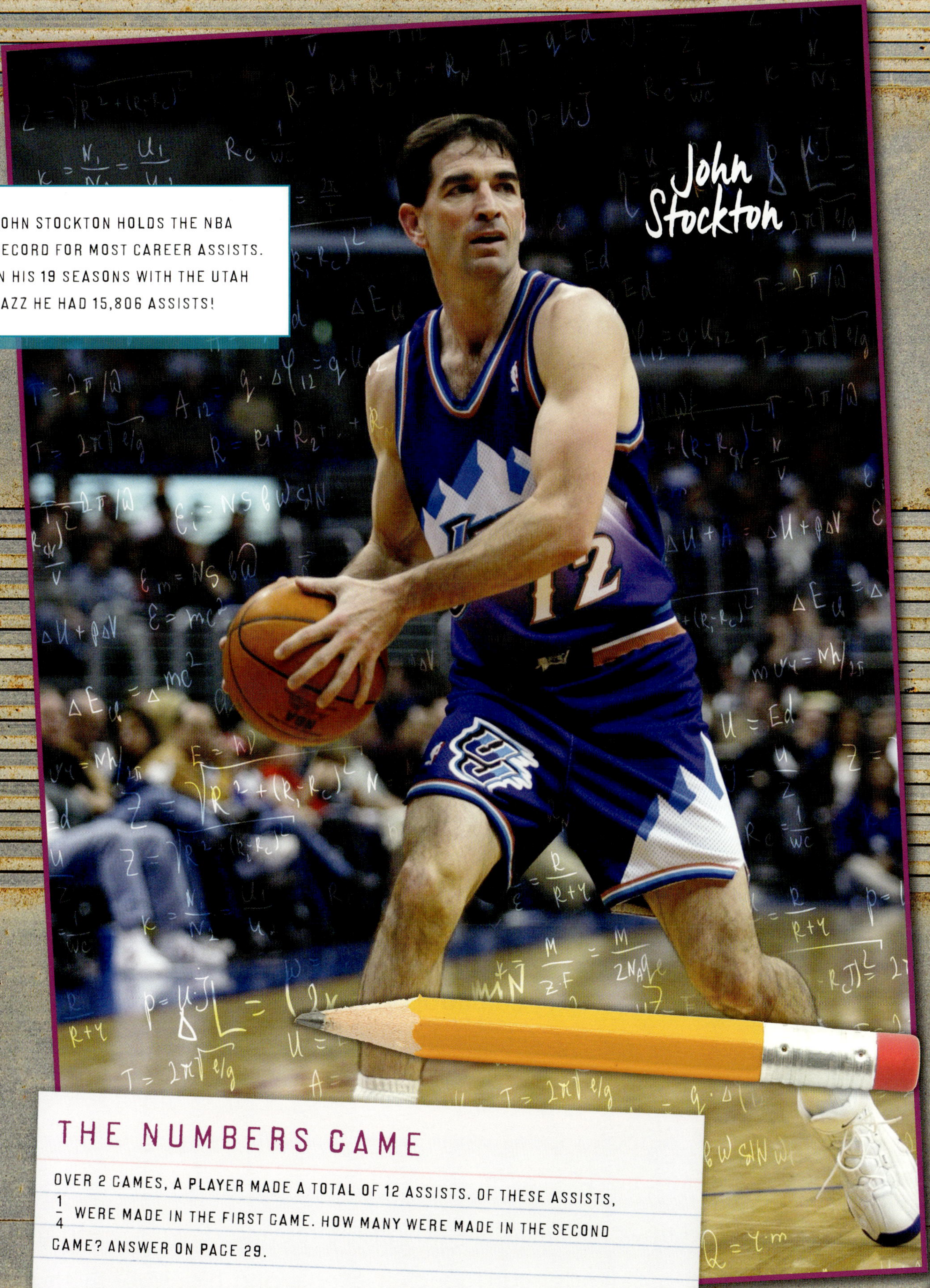

THE NUMBERS GAME

OVER 2 GAMES, A PLAYER MADE A TOTAL OF 12 ASSISTS. OF THESE ASSISTS, $\frac{1}{4}$ WERE MADE IN THE FIRST GAME. HOW MANY WERE MADE IN THE SECOND GAME? ANSWER ON PAGE 29.

Hint: $12 \times \frac{1}{4}$ *= number of assists in the first game*

Taking the ball away from a player on the other team is called stealing. When this happens, the other team gets a **turnover**. Stealing can happen by **intercepting** a pass or taking the ball away from a player while they're dribbling. Stealing gives your team another opportunity to make a shot.

A block happens when a player **deflects** a shot from going into the basket. Blocks can only happen when the ball is moving upward. Once the ball starts moving down toward the basket, a defender can't touch it. Steals and blocks both show how good a defensive player someone is.

IN THE 2015–2016 SEASON, STEPHEN CURRY MADE 169 STEALS WHILE PLAYING WITH THE GOLDEN STATE WARRIORS!

THE NUMBERS GAME

THE BEST SHOT BLOCKERS ARE OFTEN VERY TALL AND HAVE LONG ARMS. THEY CAN USUALLY JUMP HIGH AND FAST. IF A PLAYER IS 6 FEET 8 INCHES TALL, HOW MANY INCHES TALL ARE THEY TOTAL? REMEMBER, THERE ARE 12 INCHES IN A FOOT. ANSWER ON PAGE 29.

GET THE BALL

A rebound happens in basketball when a player takes possession of a ball after a shot is missed. Whichever player first takes the ball after a missed shot gets credit for the rebound. Rebounds can be either offensive or defensive.

AVERAGE STATS

Averages play a big part in basketball stats. A player's average rebounds per game can help show that they didn't just have one really good game. To figure this number out for one season, you would take the player's total rebounds and divide it by the number of games they've played.

An offensive rebound happens when the player that gets the rebound is on the same team as the player who missed the shot. This is good for their team because that means they can get a chance for another shot. A defensive rebound is when the player who gets the rebound is not on the same team as the player who shot the ball.

IN 2016, TINA CHARLES PLAYED 32 GAMES WITH THE NEW YORK LIBERTY. SHE MADE 317 REBOUNDS. THAT'S AN AVERAGE OF 9.9 REBOUNDS PER GAME!

DOUBLE STATS

Some people think the mark of a good player is if they can get their single-game stats into the double digits. If a player reaches double digits during one game in two of the five main stat **categories**—points, rebounds, assists, steals, or blocks—they get a double-double. If they get double digits in three categories, they get a triple-double!

Triple-doubles usually come from points, rebounds, and assists. Double-doubles almost always include points, but the other category usually depends on the player's size and position. It's rare for a player to make it into the double digits in steals or blocks during one game.

THE NUMBERS GAME

IT'S THE BEGINNING OF THE FOURTH QUARTER AND A PLAYER HAS ALREADY SCORED 12 POINTS! THEY'VE ALSO MADE 9 REBOUNDS AND 7 ASSISTS. IF THEY GET ONE MORE REBOUND AND TWO MORE ASSISTS, WHAT KIND OF DOUBLE WILL THEY GET? ANSWER ON PAGE 29.

TRIPLE-DOUBLES ARE HARD TO GET, BUT SOME PLAYERS, SUCH AS LEBRON JAMES, HAVE DOZENS!

MAKING IT BIG

Basketball has come a long way since it was invented more than 125 years ago. When it was first played, many of these now important statistics weren't even part of the game. Today, it's a sport ruled by the numbers. From the seconds on the clock, to the score on the board, every number matters.

THE HALL OF FAME

Hundreds of important people and players in basketball are honored in the Naismith Memorial Basketball Hall of Fame, located in Springfield, Massachusetts. Named for the man who created the sport, the Hall of Fame attracts visitors and basketball fans from all over the world!

Many players commit their lives to practicing hard and making it big in basketball. Today, a player with good stats in their high school career might go on to play basketball in college. Good stats in college could help that player someday make it to the NBA or WNBA!

ANSWER KEY

p. 7 - 4,700 square feet
p. 10 - mid-court line
p. 12 - 63 minutes
p. 17 - .480
p. 19 - 34 points
p. 21 - 9 assists
p. 23 - 80 inches
p. 26 - double-double

MOST SUCCESSFUL BASKETBALL PLAYERS STARTED OUT AS A KID WHO JUST LOVED PLAYING THE GAME!

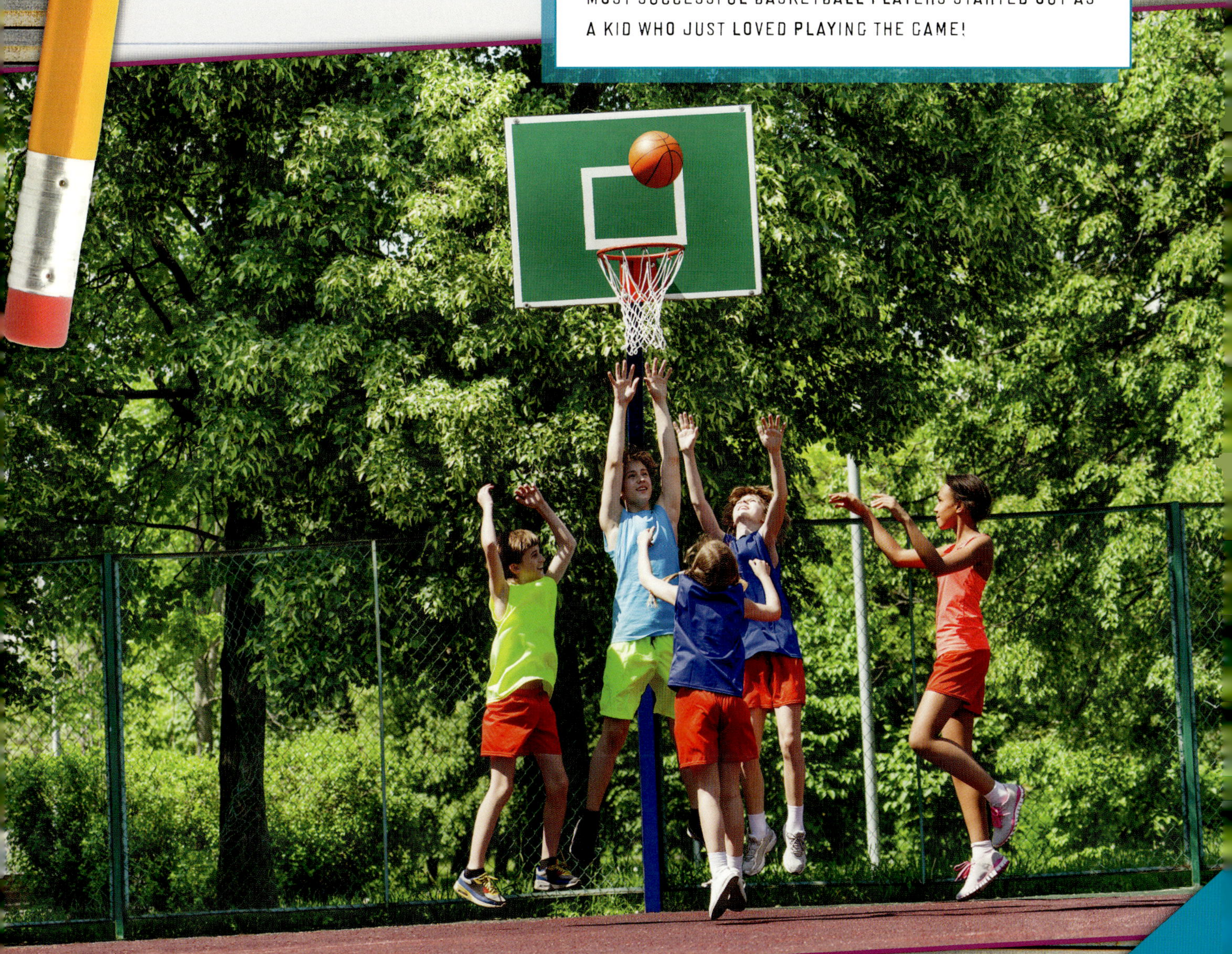

GLOSSARY

association: a group of people joined together for a purpose

calculate: to figure something out using math

category: class or group

debate: an argument

deflect: to cause something to change direction, usually by hitting it

demonstration: an act of showing something

intercept: to take control of a pass that was meant for a player on the other team

possession: having control of the ball

professional: earning money from an activity that many people do for fun

turnover: when a team loses control of the ball to the opponent

FOR MORE INFORMATION

BOOKS

Graubart, Norman D. *The Science of Basketball.* New York, NY: PowerKids Press, 2016.

Kortemeier, Todd. *Pro Basketball by the Numbers.* North Mankato, Minnesota: Capstone Press, 2016.

WEBSITES

Basic/Traditional Stats vs. Advanced Stats
jr.nba.com/basictraditional-stats-vs-advanced-stats/
This Jr. NBA page features more information on important advanced stats in basketball.

Basketball: Statistics
www.ducksters.com/sports/basketball/statistics.php
This webpage includes more facts about basketball stats and links to learn more about this exciting sport.

Publisher's note to educators and parents: Our editors have carefully reviewed these websites to ensure that they are suitable for students. Many websites change frequently, however, and we cannot guarantee that a site's future contents will continue to meet our high standards of quality and educational value. Be advised that students should be closely supervised whenever they access the Internet.

INDEX